Impossible Landscapes

Impossible Landscapes © 2005 Tony Steele.
Author photo by Jacob Steele.
Cover: illustration by Jacob Steele © 2004.
Front cover design after Jacob Steele and Lisa Marshall.
Design and in-house editing by Joe Blades.
Printed and bound in Canada by Sentinel Printing, Yarmouth NS.

Acknowledgements: Some of these poems have previously appeared in
Dialogue Through Poetry 2001 Anthology, eds. Adrian Taylor, Ram Devineni
and Lina Srivastava (New York: Rattapallax Press & Fictionopolis, 2002),
Dialogue Through Poetry 2002 Anthology, eds. Ram Devineni and Lina
Srivastava (New York: Rattapallax Press, 2003), *The Fiddlehead*, *Prairie Fire*,
The Nashwaak Review, *Spectrum*, *The Gaspereau Review*, and in the author's
previous books, *A Slanting/Line* (Santa Barbara, CA: Noel Young, 1966), and
The Dancer (Winnipeg: Wild Columbine, 1995).

Broken Jaw Press gratefully acknowledges the support of the Canada Council
for the Arts and the New Brunswick Culture and Sport Secretariat-Arts
Development Branch.

Broken Jaw Press Inc.   www.brokenjaw.com
Box 596 Stn A
Fredericton NB E3B 5A6
Canada

Library and Archives Canada Cataloguing in Publication Data

Steele, Tony, 1935-
    Impossible landscapes : poems narrative and lyrical / Tony Steele.

ISBN 1-55391-037-0

I. Title.

PS8537.T433I56 2005   C811'.54   C2005-902354-6

Impossible Landscapes
Poems Narrative and Lyrical

TONY STEELE

Fredericton • Canada

Impossible Landscapes

BORDER CROSSINGS

IMPOSSIBLE LANDSCAPES

Impossible Landscapes

i

as in a dream
or on a scroll
with a brush drawing

we sit in the mouth
of our tent
on a
rainy day
high
in Sentinel Pass
gazing down
through the
mist
at the
frozen
lake

ii

the sun feels hot
in the thin air
as we pick our way
through the scree
up the pass
and along the saddle
towards Mt. Temple
we talk little
but pass the
water bottle
back and forth
gratefully

Still More Impossible Landscapes

i

the snow was heavier
above the tree line
we weren't prepared
for the climb
to sentinel pass

didn't even consider it

I was cast as
group leader
and moral center
the position
exceedingly lonely
especially at night

ii

I had my own tent
which was good and bad
private but cold
wake up at five
and inhale the frost
longing carefully
for an invisible embrace

burning with the paradox
of loneliness without being
able to be alone
I dreamed of watching
the mountains crumble

iii

there were other dreams
erotic mostly as I remember
in one I seduced my absent lover
by reciting the opening lines
of Chaucer's *Caunterbury Tales*
She kissed me passionately—
as we lay of a bed—
more keenly than almost ever in life

another night Brigitte Bardot
comes to a writer's conference
dressed in the bulky sweater
she wears to conceal
the famous breasts of her movie days
I long to tell her I have always admired
her beauty and idealism
and her fidelity to principle

she is under attack
by the other writers
only I appreciate her
Jan Horner and Doug Smith
have a fight ending
in her slugging him and
knocking him out
neither of them resembles
the real persons
who bear
their names

these dreams leave me dissatisfied
with what remains with me awake

iv

on Big Beehive
it was cold
out of season
but we'd brought
acrylics and watercolours
so we shivered
as we painted
our views of Lake Louise
from above

The Walking Bridges at Fredericton

we roll over the Saint John
over that vastness of regattas
under the central suicide arch
look upstream at the old train bridge
with eddies swirling around its derelict butts
with their nests of swallows—
on either side

                    upstart and weathered villages

but on the bridge over the Nashwaak
still untamed with its brackish water
and brown weeds below the surface

we park our bikes and lean our heads
out over the edge of this slim passage
from one emptiness to another

On a Trail Below Camino Cielo

Larry and David ran on
down the trail around
an abrupt
turn which brought them to the gorge

facing inaccessible
lunar and snow
covered peaks
that gave them a lesson in

space and sent them running back
to me with distance
and cold wind
burning their faces the first time

THE GUERRERO POEMS

Guerrero Descending the Mountain

i—Guerrero's Departure

Guerrero knew it was time
to slip down the canyon
to the coastal valley

he could see smoke from the fires
of the government troops
beyond the ridge

tomorrow or the next day
the woods would be aflame
time to go

he tore up his last papers
and burned them in the grate
and stared after

the ashes had long crumbled
he packed rice and trailfood
with some peppers

from the garden, tied them to
his fighting staff, looked once
at the cabin

and started down the creek bed
dry and full of boulders
towards the city

ii—The Rebellion

it started with a political pretext
something about Mao, something about
Fidel, or land reform or Che
as if we were a region of peasants

as usual principle altered itself
until it was no more than looting
pillage, rape, murder, defilement
revenge for forgotten insults

and the loyalists were no better
again as usual shooting hostages
indiscriminately "to make an example"
filling the slough with carrion

now the factions are uncountable
the survivors are armed or gone to ground
fires smoulder in the ruins
of stately houses given back to the chaparral

iii—Guerrero Leaves the Cabin

the fire was moving down the mountain
sweeping across the chaparral
and leaping in gusts between the live oaks
below in the coastal plain the city
was burning neighborhood by neighborhood
orchestrated by bursts of automatic rifle fire
from up here you could not see
who were the loyalists and who the rebels
at the second bend of the down canyon trail
Guerrero took a last look at the cabin
nested in woods its porch framed by bougainvillea
vibrating in thermal waves
seated there as if nothing could ever
happen to it again. he felt a rush of well-being
and trudged off down the trail

iv—Guerrero Descending

the way down is
more difficult
than the ascent
            would be
to go
up the mountain
            means
only to put one foot after
the other till
you reach the top

to go down you
must use your brain
choose where to put each step beware
of sudden falls
and moraine

Guerrero watched
the ground as he walked and
before he knew it
was down among the sycamores

v—Guerrero in Rattlesnake Canyon

the going is rougher
between the boulders
cast up by the spring floods

but the trail is lost
in underbrush
tangles of poison oak

the popcorn blossoms
of ceanothus and manzanita
between the rocks and the little stream

there are no rattlesnakes here
only up near the pass
where they are roasting by now

despite the fire and wind
it is cool in the gorge
and the way relentlessly downwards

vi—Guerrero on the Joy of Battle

unreal today—the war at three removes
with guns that make holes in strangers
too far away to see the colour of their faces
the real battle was always a dream fight
with hands and feet in slow motion
at whatever speed, one's force
springing from the earth, from the legs
through the hips, the twist of the
torso and shoulders and
finally to the fist
"I punch with my feet" said Guerrero

vii—Guerrero on Marriage

Guerrero was married
a couple of times
before the revolution

he had some thoughts
on that subject—take
a good look at the mother

and aunts of your woman
think what you can do
for yourself and what you

might need from someone else:
you may want to perform
the morning coffee ceremony alone

viii—His Memories of the Cabin

it was an age ago
we sat on the floor
trying our voices
against the hum of bees

or sat apart
not wanting anything

my pack is full of maps
of all the places we went
together—it would all be
so easy now
and impossible

ix—His Tiger Mask

is all animal
you cannot see
behind its eyes

though you see much
and see through much
you cannot see
behind its eyes

His Memories of Elizabeth

it was free
so we all
took as much
as we wanted

Then they started to charge for it so he used more and
more saving his allowances of nickels and dimes in a jar
on the dresser and afterwards in bills under the mattress
when he was becoming affluent. But of course by that
time the price had gone up again.

That was before he met Elizabeth. Her gestures paralyzed
him. As when she lifted her long shimmering hair above
her head and let it fall in a bright landslide along her neck
and shoulders. Then she would press her shoulder blades
against the back of her seat to make sure he would see
the pert nipples of her small drooping breasts against the
rough cotton of her man's shirt . . . or an inch or two of
pale skin at the waist. Once she sat opposite him with her
jeans spread to show him the patch of flowers sewn on
just where the legs meet.

now the house
is cold and
mildewed
as expected

She would disappear for weeks and then she would be
at his side touching his leg as if by accident, chattering
about her mother who was now in town, now on a ranch
in Saskatchewan. She spoke of her mother with awe. "My
mother lives on the ranch now. I want to spend Christmas
with her." He thinks, "I want to ask you more about your
mother but I've lost you again. When will I see you again,
as I saw you then? Even the very letters of your name are
hard to form in my mouth: e-l-i-z-a-b-e-t-h . . .

"But you come much later in the story, Elizabeth. Sit
there and polish your nails, read a book or something, and
I will come back to you later."

now we pay
for each thing
we once wanted
too much

and now in your eyes
I am like my name
when I come to you
from life's battleground

Guerrero Revisits the Mountain

Guerrero went back up the mountain
after the dust storm, or shit storm—
—it depends on your point of view
—the revolution was over suddenly
and things returned to normal
                    everybody said
the mountain fell on the valley—the corpses
had been removed from the slough
traffic was allowed again but there were no cars
only pedestrians and a few bikes
Painted Cave was burned out:
a few live oaks survived
and masses of wildflowers that lie dormant
except after great fires

the cabin was no more—ashes and cinders
a bulldozer had buried Guerrero's hidey-hole
under a of ton of clay
his careful stash lies safe
until some millennial
anthropologist
digs it up and carefully
arrays the plastic bags
and desiccated leaves
as relics of culture-ways
[dating approximate, class
and ritual links uncertain]

well, nothing to do here
he thought—the old fighter
turned away and continued up the pass

Guerrero Heads East

Guerrero crossed the pass
of Santa Ynez through a notch
between two glacial boulders
he sat on one for a drink
and a look down both valleys:
the coastal plain he was leaving
and the narrow valley of orchards
to which he was descending

looking east he saw the next ridge
and the blue shadow of the ridge beyond

on a path of pine needles
cool in the shade
of the afternoon sun
he set off for a distant sea

the whole continent lay ahead of him
its peaks and plains seemed still
perhaps full of unknown
peoples who fled the wars

as he left the tree covering
his lengthening shadow pointed
towards the Great Plains
site of future mystery

He Reaches the Foothills

Guerrero has crossed the mountains
a chain of picture postcard opportunities
a story told often enough
(sleeping rough, eating
roots and berries
drinking tepid high altitude
tea . . . and all that)

in a foothills tavern
he rests from the sun
and watches cowboys
punch VLT machines
—this is a new country
at peace with itself
heedless of the wars
as if the western coast
were not in flames

he doesn't know who he is
anymore. He feels like
a time traveler in
a TV drama or
Hollywood movie:
Kung Fu meets *Gone*
with the Wind
he asks the bartender
about a room
for the night
as he sips
a cold draught

Jugarse: Body and Soul
—for Bob Thompson

his body is a certain red
like a flaming shadow
matching the colour
of her mane and pubis

this in a green valley
where Guerrero passed
between one descent
and another—these lovers

gleamed immensely
above the landscape
embodiments
of his secret wish

suddenly his world
was in flames—he lay
in the heat of a steamy
afternoon, his tongue

touching that purple
birthmark on blue freckled
skin—from her throat
to just above a nipple

OTHER LANDSCAPES

Savage Harbour

Fireweed burns coolly under
a northeast wind off the gulf.
Yesterday they looked so hot
and dry I thought they'd explode.
The sea shakes its stone prison
as the fireweed break loose from
their open meadow and spill

into the surrounding bay-
berry/rose territory.
There's a wildness here I
could not control if I wished—
a war—the wild grasses steal
a march on the saskatoons and
nothing grows back where someone

bulldozed a road and sketched a
turnaround area be-
tween the house and the last cliffs
before the wildest battle
begins on the very shore
where moment by moment loss
and gain and struggle prevail.

Prairie Landscape

his version
we stand inside an immense circle—
that clump of trees is not the true rim
of the world only some bush gone wild
that protects a farm now sinking in the soil

this imagined circle has no true centre though
the weather-worn boards of the ruined farm
imply a centre—we want to map the world
around hearths even where they are not

the broken, crooked radii on which we walk
stagger outwards from one nothing to another
we desert no truly human homestead
as we voyage outward dream-driven and empty

her version
children played here once—I hear their bones
twist under the wormy sod—the air is dry.
Just now and over there are two streams
that meander underground to that river
beyond the hill almost at the edge of sight
all around us—I breathe the secret springs
bubbling up almost to the prairie grass
oozing between the legs of the fallen ones
sowed on these plains before the plows—
they gave birth in these invisible waters
moaned ecstatic cries and set loose the children
who now play hide-and-seek beneath my feet

A Familiar Landscape

—in the country beyond the rivers
is a landscape of landscapes
a perfect place of changes

i

my uncle Guy painted miniatures
tiny nudes, landscapes, bowls
of flowers, and velvet gowns
abstract patterns of crumpled
      cigarette papers
he also made portraits
by artificial light
of famous men and biblical
heroes painted with wax in
      reverse on protectoid

he found his subjects in the streets
and Automats of New York City
what he called cafeteria society
Moses was a gutter bum
      and Naomi a bag lady

ii

Corinn my aunt
painted by daylight
in large formats
—a jack-in-the-pulpit
as big as a tree

she called back the defunct
buildings of her childhood
—a village in Wisconsin
with a mill and general store
and a few dozen scrambly houses

the nineteenth century frontier became
a lurid watercolour
devoid of human figures
sinking quickly back to earth
menaced by gigantic plants

iii

in New York they rented
a west side studio
the room too small
for them to work together

she used the daylight
while he rambled the city
he painted at night
by electric lamp

they laid the drawing board
flat on a packing crate
at mealtime and covered
it with a linen cloth

candles and fine food
a life of paint and sharing
of piquant intimacy
of peace, love and work

From the Hampton Shore

weathered floats
washed up on the shore
hang from the railing of the deck

the land dips to a sea
that moves in its cage
easing forth fifty years

of flotsam that brings
forgetfulness
before thunderheads on the rim

fifty years is a leaf
falling in a vast woods:
the brain sputters into flight—

as these summer days
fool us into everlastingness—
saying no until the end

Vacancies

we are driving across Canada in a smooth white car
at a fixed rate, the pine trees turn into miles
bored with the vacancies and the tunnel vision highway
we rest in ruggedly pruned forests
by noble rivers with waterfalls
                     articulate birds
             and basso profundo frogs
we greet fellow travellers in gas stations
                                       and camps
comparing notes on weather and insects

where are the stories in this endless landscape?
the stories are hidden in the forests and
in battered houses almost out of sight
                   on the wrong side of the road
to learn these stories you must hide
in the landscape until you too are almost lost
we pass on through moving easily
                   toward our destination

The Coming of Dionysus

was the sea always this same blue?
      she asks even as she sees his sail
            turn the headland and make for the beach

the god cruises shoreward with drums
      cornets flagons flights of sparrows
            whirling round the mast

the sea no longer blue
      she knows not what to call these shades
            the colours of Olympus at last

despite confusion of her mind
      her body walks gaily
            through the surf in greeting

but it is not Dionysus who comes
      only the sunset as usual
            divinely coloured perhaps

this is the final humiliation:
      she hangs herself upon the tree
            that to this day bears her name

The Solar Point of View

You are right in saying that Hoon is Hoon although
it could be that he is the son of old man Hoon.
He sounds like a Dutchman. I think the word is
probably an automatic cipher for "the loneliest air,"
that is to say, the expanse of sky and space.
—Wallace Stevens, *Letters*

I am the light behind reality
falling through the western sky
a breeder of planets—not unique
but only the neighborhood star.

The hero is a lonely man
in the fields of Mars or hid
lugubriously in his tent
cause and solution of the war.

What does he think, Theseus,
when he leaves her on that island?
Going out for a cup of coffee,
telling her you'll be back soon.

Knowing she would wait for you,
like Odysseus, the outcast
of the universe. Until some rainy day
you return like a bad dream.

Theseus, of course, doesn't hang about.
Having more adventures to fulfill,
He's not to be found on the next island
or the one after that. The man is gone.

Ariadne waits long as she can bear.
She watches the sea for a sail or sign.
But all she finds is me and I am nothing,
or perhaps the knowing behind the thing.

Flying Home

Flying through the dark
compressed into a chair
you picture the pilots
with their instruments
also flying through the dark.

This experience is well arranged
by others: as if they knew
where you were going to.

You hope you will arrive
at a home familiar and strange.

You approach the airport.
Flaps lower: you feel
an urgency in the dip of a wing.

The window reflects your face
and you see the lights
of the landing strip,

feel the drag of gravity. You say
the names of your children, one by one
I love you, each one of you—
how much? Oh, completely
—as if you will ever know

Existential Fears

Death

Our alphabet begins with D.
D is for death and for denial.
As far ahead as we can see,
Rescue lasts only for a while.

Born with this fear we awaken screaming
Fighting for air in long hard breaths.
For decades then we live by dreaming,
Unconscious among a thousand deaths.

Sooner or later we will find
Courageous masquerades must end.
Unknowable fears control the mind
And emptiness waits around the bend.

Isolation

The winter landscape blackens the pines
Across the half-plowed fields of snow.
The watcher at the window notes the lines
Of power wires and their shadows below.

The days are getting longer now,
But still he wakes before the light.
He observes a blue jay on a bough,
And counts again the hours until night.

There are some footprints in the snow,
And nailed-bootgrips in his brain,
But whose they are he does not know—
As he looks, waits, and continues sane.

Freedom

He has no reason to stay here but
Still he remains in every weather.
He looks for an impulse in his gut
To flee, or hold his world together.

The world is open. He can go
Back to where he came from once
Or to a place he doesn't' know—
Tomorrow or in a couple of months.

He'll strike out down the random road,
Seeking places merely far,
Or any site that breaks the code
Of staying in touch with where you are.

Meaninglessness

Of all the fears the easiest one
To take is the universal state
Where things fall by fortune alone—
A world controlled by luck and fate.

And he can find no fault in this,
This view that life is lacking sense.
Why worry if nothing can be amiss
In going forth and coming hence?

He counts his blessings, chiefly this:
He never learned to worship gods.
The question to ask from where he is,
Is not what it means but what are the odds?

BORDER CROSSINGS

Six Very Short Poems

Sleepless
Tunnel beneath the mountain,
listen to a faucet drip.

Autumn
Yellow tree, red tree
a checkerboard along the street.
This could be the last game.

Hoople
The professor nodded and smiled
as he denied my words.

Time
I haven't felt this old
for years.

Zeno's Paradox
You paralyze the brains of those
innocent of infinity.

Silence
Nothing can wall this in.

Selected States of Mind
—an autobiographical geography of America

i
Today my mind is
like New Mexico
high and flat
with mesas bisected
with arroyos and discrete
mud-coloured cliff houses
mostly it thinks in Spanish

ii
But yesterday it was
Michigan—two huge peninsulas
reach out to each other
never expecting to touch

iii
Saturday is California
with its peaks of ice and
multitudes of hipsters
we carry our boards down
to the shore and regard the surf
through the early morning mist
everyday should be Saturday

iv
Sunday is a small town
in New England
Massachusetts say
Neat white churches surrounded
by parked cars and gravestones
all the shops are closed
but there's a picnic in the park

v
In Rhode Island
I am the epitome
of insignificance

vi
As a Yankee
in South Carolina
I embrace
lost causes
that I can
never approve

vii
I am a child learning
to spell the name
*M*IS-*S*IS-*S*IPP*I*
Poverty and power
together
place of lynchings
and William Faulkner

viii

Here in Wisconsin
is the birthplace
of my mother
and of my romance
with nature
I paddle my canoe
among the treetops
of a drowned river

ix

Washington is a favourite
alternative life
where I walk beside
the sound with a
different set of children
and dream my way to Asia
beyond the Olympic Peninsula

x

I am off most people's map
here in North Dakota
prairies and badlands
ranging cattle rivers in flood
Americans think of this
as being the Far North

xi

I am as ornery as a townsman
of northern Maine
far from the hype of Bar Harbor
and Acadia National Park
in Gardiner I worship at the shrine
of Edwin Arlington Robinson
and abjure all easy solutions

xii

I feel my age today
like the Atlantic coast
of Florida land of the aged
we watch the sea
from our tall condos
and plan our lunches
across the Inland Waterway

xiii

The rebellious state
of New Albion
surrounded the bay.
We marched and chanted
to set us apart
from angelic inversions
and theme parks of the south.

My Life With Food

in those days
we ate and drank and smoked
without regrets
as if there were no war or race riots
or murder of the innocents

chopped liver for the soul
corn-rye with caraway seed
and matzoh balls
made from scratch

raw ground round steak
on slabs of country bread
with salt, pepper and raw onions

Harold set the house record
fifty-two raw green onions
consumed before dinner
chased down with whiskey

fried chicken liver and eggs
with toasted bagel

sweetbreads sautéed in butter
with fresh green beans and a baked potato

Porterhouse steaks
marinated with lemon and onions
grilled in the fireplace
on a driftwood fire
—black on the outside
just warm within

Harold sits by the fire
stroking Rose's head
telling her what beautiful hair she has
and insisting on just one more drink
before driving back to Detroit

Sunday morning
in my parents' bedroom
eating Chinese takeout
listening to the radio comedies
(Duffy's Tavern where the elite meet to eat/
Archie the manager speaking/
Duffy ain't here)
interrupted by a special announcement:
that's how I remember Pearl Harbor

starving and dehydrating
to make the weight for Saturday morning
—afterwards a bottle of honey
before the match

a hunk of cheddar
a ripe tomato
a bottle of Old Vienna
(the handsome waiter)
I watch the sky turn purple
as a tornado approaches
across the indigo lake

Palimpsest

what is near is far tonight
vaguely roaming through the dark
trees at the edge of the park
are burning in the moonlight

young Annabelle sweet and all
leans against the poplar tree
and turns her back to me
by the burnt-down dance hall

her freckles, her short red hair
tangy as the night we met
are steeped in summer and in sweat
her T-shirt loose, her navel bare

but now again it's only today
the first times were always best
but now again it's only today
and only words to say are left

what is near is far tonight
vaguely roaming through the dark
trees at the edge of the park
are burning in the moonlight
trees at the edge of the park
are burning in the moonlight

My Parents' Garden

In the cottage garden
her columbines sprouted
at home in the city
flaunt their hybrid blue

He plucks a pink and white
bachelor button
for his collar
and departs to forage
for antiques

I enter the woods
in search of paintbrush
the indian campground
the central tulip tree
and in sandy soil
along forest paths
the miniature world
of wild columbines

His Return to Rondeau

He turns off Highway 3 at Morpeth
and threads the neck of land to the peninsula.
Early May: hazy light through the young leaves.
Geese and goslings float on the bay.
He notes a B&B in a stone farmhouse by the slough,
a subdivision just before the park,
a standard Ontario Parks Service kiosk.
The miniature golf course, neglected since 1940,
is gone, as is the dance pavilion
and the old general store and the superintendent's house.
The pier and yacht club remain but need painting.
The park feels more organized today,
with signs and maps and names for every trail.

He drives along the lakeshore (one mile
from the cottage to the store, as he recalls).
Most of the old cottages remain with a few
gaps like missing teeth. He searches for
the old numbers among the new 911s.
But 212 is missing. He recognizes
the pines on which hung a rope swing.
The small circular car park
is overgrown. He looks in vain for rocks
from his mother's garden and sticks
from the cottage, apparently vanished
tracelessly . . .
On a half-dead apple tree he finds
a withered crab from last season.
He walks to the beach on the weedy path
past bird houses on poles.
His childhood home is now a sanctuary.

Before dinner they would gather driftwood
to roast steaks marinated with onions and lemon juice,
singed on the outside by the high flames in the stone fireplace,
and served on the porch with fresh tomatoes and beer.

The lake is calm and misty
He chooses some fragments
of driftwood for souvenirs.

Back at the site of the cottage
the view is as empty as before.
The other buildings look smaller
and more faded than his memories.

He has visited this place many times
in his dreams. In these the water
is much higher than now.
The house remains, inhabited
by a soft-voiced dark woman.
He walks up the flowered pathway
to her door. They regard each other
through the screen. She invites him in.
The door begins to open as the dream ends.

Questions of Spiritual Materialism

*The problem is that ego can convert anything to its
own use, even spirituality.*
—Chögyam Trungpa

What workman built the beds
that fit inside the cabin rooms?
Whose shoulders did he stand upon
to see the landscapes
of his insatiable ambitions?
On what river bridge was he born?
What scurvied child hammered the last
to shape his brand name running shoes?
What grease saturated tenements
housed the builders of his sleek machines?
How many lived in stinking poverty
so he could perform Tai Chi in the park?

These queries
and other static
revolved in his brain.
He sat observing
his exhalations
and his inhalations.
When the questions arose
he labeled them as thoughts.

On the other side of the planet
a child was crossing a mountain pass
and descending into a green valley
between the moraines of receding glaciers.

Contact Sheets

the pictures are all
much alike
blurs of silvery
black and white
until with magnifying glass
the differences arise
to meet your eyes

one out of ten—
a good ratio
of shots to save
but the sheet itself—
seen altogether—shapes
its own kind of picture

a photo made of photos
of something about to happen
the figure of the fool
looking at eternity—
as he's on the point of
stepping over the cliff
a white dog nips his heels

Isla Vista Beach

that was a day once when I walked into it:
up the stairs and along the balcony
to the door #69 and right on in

through the door and everything—
all the stuff—was lying in a plain
ceramic bowl on the coffee table

and then the walking started
down the labourer's path between
the unfinished apartment bldgs

to the sea—first the cliffs—
low tide! out on the sand flats
to the rocks—seagrass like

hair covering the genitals
of immense hermaphrodites
with chemical bodies

long blond legs playing in the ruins
of a druid's circle rusted
in the surf: gun emplacement
or observation tower—no one
remembers—a defunct observatory
sea home of invertebrates laid open

. . . day stretches wide like low tide
hello darkness falling purple
around the cypresses at Devereux Point

—back at #69—different jazz
on the record player, closed room
outside the night, starts, no moon
illuminated sky, the closed room
unknown dancers, never seen again
so many of them never seen again

The Yachts

*It's the time of the year
And the time of the day.*
—Wallace Stevens

The Start
the smooth crumbled stone
of the breakwater Sunday
afternoon before a race

a sail luffing, a sail
racing seaward—the crew
bent over his stopwatch

the fat judges' boat bobbing
on the line, with red white and blue
flags opposite a rusty buoy

Outward Bound
helm down hard on
port tack the fleet
inshore to starboard

the wind fresh
in the channel
at the moment

when we can see
past Campus Point
we'll come about

and reach the far buoy
first if we guessed right
if the wind doesn't change

    The Far Buoy
close enough!
we tack in front
of the lead boat

the sheet lashed
to my wrist
leaning out

I can smell
sea scum
on iron

as we heel
tight into
the buoy

    Finish
the wind shifts
we plod before it
bouncing on swells

these bright new boats
have passed us
as we slither home

the palms by the breakwater
grow tall again
festooned with flags

Chamomile

The chamomile grows wild
in the cracks of the sidewalk.
A member of the daisy family,
we called it *pineapple weed*
for its conical central hive
that when rubbed between your fingers
smelled like fresh cut golden fruit.

High in the castle on Mountain Drive
we drink a pot of chamomile
to settle our nerves as we gaze
down the valley past the streets of town
at the plains of Goleta dissolving
in coastal fog with only
the central peak
       of Anacapa
           visible
           just above.

In the A-Frame on Coyote Road

by firelight and candlelight
I hear Erik Satie for the first time
and lubricated by a quart of York Mountain Red
we play go through the night
mindful of the black widows
living in the hearth

at first the black stones look best
in time you learn to prefer
the better gamesman's white stones

go like life requires virtue
greed loses in the end
the most esthetic move
is also the winning play

today in another country
I see the men and women
like black and white stones
on a gleaming board

Giving Up by the Goleta Slough

I trail behind the others down the grassy path
from the cliffs to the beach. The world
like a woman's body, a woman's body like
the imitation of an earth. I pause and look
back into the folds of the ravines
at the curled, hairy, dry brush
around the sides of the canyon.
Where the path opens to the rock-piled beach,
I see the only red flower on the path.
And near it a yellow mushroom.

I don't remember when I first started abdicating.
But now I am no longer a writer and interested only
in making sure each word is different, the paper
begins to look holy again. It looks like the yellow
sheets of rough draft my aunt composed
in my sister's bedroom when I was twelve:
the product of a magic brain, no longer entirely my own.

I can tell when the moment of sunset has come
when the silver tops of the olive trees turn dark.

My Travels in Santa Barbara County

In Solvang we watch a Dane work
with a shovel in the sun to build a car store
where he will buy a car when the man pays him.
He is glistening brown from sun and sweat.
He sustains himself against the sun
by thinking about the muscles in his back.

Nothing ever happens. That's the truth.
Or, nothing ever happens outside,
everything happens inside, like seeing.

A young blond girl in a man's shirt
stands beside the body of a VW
and shows me her ingenuous smile.
Another walking her bicycle
looks at me steadily as she passes
with a slight widening of the eyes.

I'm in Alameda Park
under the Rousseau trees
from the Canary Islands.
The shadows are moving in.
Though I tremble I am not afraid.
The people walking their dogs,
playing at Frisbee, sitting in their cars,
are assemblages of light.

Sharon stands under a mimosa tree.
She holds a blossom between the second
and third fingers of her right hand.

Vomito ergo sum. My puke reminds me
that I am alive. I breathed some of it today.

I wear my old leather jacket tonight
because it has been with me everywhere.
I want to live in the park.
I was raised to live in parks.
I have been happy in parks.
Today I orbited one of my larger circles
in a truck collecting nostalgias.

Saw men like statues, statues like men.

Everything solid feels good
like the crack in this table.
I hold it tightly with four finger tips.

What did you have for dinner?
Cottage cheese, cherries, and fritos.

What did you eat later when you took a walk
down State Street to the Rice Bowl?
A bowl of rice.

How does the passage of time seem now?
Miraculous and unrelated to the order of incidents.

Thank you. What's the cause?
The non-relatedness of time began
when the great clock stopped.

I can see the darkness in the trees.
And when I see the bench I see
that what I said was true.
Everything is different.

Today I saw a funeral with neatly dressed mourners.
I saw people of all ages. A lady by her car told her companion,
with gestures, about the blisters on her calf.

I saw the moon light up over the palm trees in the park.
The Rousseau trees droop menacingly.
I feel the first cool night breeze, hear the high whine
of Japanese motorcycles above other traffic sounds.

I believe that each word should be different.
That is my principle of style.

On the Beach at Night

A pigeon flies over and shits on my left shoulder.
"It's a nice saffron colour," says Gordon,
"the shade Buddhists use for their robes,
colour of the fires of spiritual abnegation."
And it's also the colour of pigeon shit.

I take off my shirt and walk away
from this smear of thought,
this flurry of conversation.

For no reason words come clearly now:
It's like standing on the beach at night
and watching the luminescent waves
emerge from the blankness of the ocean.
I know they originate out there.
But I cannot see or hear through the darkness.

A Selection of Our Titles in Print

A Fredericton Alphabet. John Leroux, photos, architecture, 1-896647-77-4
Afterimage / накнадна слика. Joe Blades, Bobana Stephen, translator, poetry, 1-55391-016-8
All the Perfect Disguises. Lorri Neilsen Glenn, poetry, 1-55391-010-9
Antimatter. Hugh Hazelton, poetry, 1-896647-98-7
Avoidance Tactics. Sky Gilbert, drama, 1-896647-50-2
Break the Silence. Denise DeMoura, poetry, 1-896647-87-1
Crossroads Cant. Grace, Seabrook, Shafiq, Shin. Joe Blades, editor, poetry, 0-921411-48-0
Cuerpo amado / Beloved Body. Nela Rio; Hugh Hazelton, translator, poetry, 1-896647-81-2
Dancing Alone: Selected Poems. William Hawkins, poetry, 1-55391-034-6
Day of the Dog-tooth Violets. Christina Kilbourne, short fiction, 1-896647-44-8
During Nights That Undress Other Nights / En las noches que desvisten otras noches. Nela Rio; Elizabeth Gamble Miller, translator, poetry, 1-55391-008-7
Garden of the Gods. Dina Desveaux, novel, 1-55391-016-4
Great Lakes logia. Joe Blades, editor, art & writing anthology, 1-896647-70-7
Groundswell: the best of above/ground press, 1993-2003. rob mclennan, editor, poetry, 1-55391-012-5
Herbarium of Souls. Vladimir Tasić, short fiction, 0-921411-72-3
Impossible Landscapes. Tony Steele, poetry, 1-55391-037-0
Jive Talk: George Fetherling in Interviews and Documents. Joe Blades, ed., 1-896647-54-5
Let Rest. Serge Patrice Thibodeau; Jonathan Kaplansky, translator, 1-55391-035-4
Mangoes on the Maple Tree. Uma Parameswaran, fiction, 1-896647-79-0
Manitoba highway map. rob mclennan, poetry, 0-921411-89-8
Memories of Sandy Point, St George's Bay, Newfoundland. Phyllis Pieroway, social history, 1-55391-029-X
Maiden Voyages. Scott Burke, editor, drama, 1-55391-023-0
Paper Hotel. rob mclennan, poetry, 1-55391-004-4
Peppermint Night. Vanna Tessier, poetry, 1-896647-83-9
Postcards from Ex-Lovers. Jo-Anne Elder, fiction, 1-55391-036-2
Reader Be Thou Also Ready. Robert James, fiction, 1-896647-26-X
Republic of Parts. Stephanie Maricevic, poetry, 1-55391-025-7
resume drowning. Jon Paul Fiorentino, poetry, 1-896647-94-4
Shadowy Technicians: New Ottawa Poets. rob mclennan, editor, poetry, 0-921411-71-5
Song of the Vulgar Starling. Eric Miller, poetry, 0-921411-93-6
Speaking Through Jagged Rock. Connie Fife, poetry, 0-921411-99-5
Starting from Promise. Lorne Dufour, poetry, 1-55391-026-5
Sunset. Pablo Urbanyi; Hugh Hazelton, translator, fiction, 1-55391-014-1
Sustaining the Gaze / Sosteniendo la mirada / Soutenant le regard. Brian Atkinson, Nela Rio; Elizabeth Gamble Miller, Jill Valery, translators, photo essay, poetry, 1-55391-028-1
Sweet Mother Prophesy. Andrew Titus, fiction, 1-55391-002-8
Tales for an Urban Sky. Alice Major, poetry, 1-896647-11-1
The Longest Winter. Julie Doiron, Ian Roy, photos, short fiction, 0-921411-95-2
The Robbie Burns Revival & Other Stories. Cecilia Kennedy, short fiction, 1-55391-024-9
The Space of Light / El espacio de la luz. Nela Rio; Elizabeth Gamble Miller, editor and translator, short fiction and poetry, 1-55391-020-6
The Sweet Smell of Mother's Milk-Wet Bodice. Uma Parameswaran, fiction, 1-896647-72-3
The Yoko Ono Project. Jean Yoon, drama, 1-55391-001-X
This Day Full of Promise. Michael Dennis, poetry, 1-896647-48-0
Túnel de proa verde / Tunnel of the Green Prow. Nela Rio; Hugh Hazelton, translator, poetry, 1-896647-10-3
What Was Always Hers. Uma Parameswaran, short fiction, 1-896647-12-X

www.brokenjaw.com hosts our current catalogue, submissions guidelines, manuscript award competitions, booktrade sales representation and distribution information. Directly from us, all individual orders must be prepaid. All Canadian orders must add 7% GST/HST. CRA Number: 892667403RT0001. Broken Jaw Press Inc., Box 596 Stn A, Fredericton NB E3B 5A6, Canada.